BRICK TEXTURE

12 SHEETS SINGLE-SIDED
SCRAPBOOKING DESIGNS FOR CRAFTS

SCRAPBOOK PAPER PAD
6x6, NON-PERFORATED SHEETS

© Crafty As Ever

To remove cut along the dotted line.

To remove cut along the dotted line.

www.ingramcontent.com/pod-product-compliance
Lightning Source LLC
Chambersburg PA
CBHW042141030726
47599CB00002B/569